KILL THE RENT
GROW YOUR BIZ

KILL THE RENT
GROW YOUR BIZ

FIVE SIMPLE STEPS TO CUT COSTS, ATTRACT MORE CLIENTS & IMPROVE YOUR BOTTOM LINE

L.D. HOWARD

Disclaimer:

The advice and strategies found within may not be suitable for every situation. This work is produced and sold with the understanding that neither the author nor the publisher are held responsible for the results accrued from the advice in this book.

Copyright © 2018 by Howard Corporate Centre, LLC.
All rights reserved.

No portion of this book may be reproduced, stored in a retrieval system, or transmitted in any form or by any means — electronic, mechanical, photocopying, recording, scanning, or other — except for brief quotations in critical reviews or articles, without the prior written permission of the publisher.

ISBN-13: 978-1985197282
ISBN-10: 1985197286

DEDICATION

This book is dedicated to the clients of Howard Corporate Centre, LLC — past, present and future. Thank you for entrusting the Centre to support your business. In my view, there is no greater honor and privilege that an entrepreneur can have than to realize a dream whose sole purpose is to help other entrepreneurs realize theirs.

This book is also dedicated to my parents for their support in helping to make Howard Corporate Centre, LLC a reality. We've had a lot of lumps, bumps — and laughs — during the past six years, and the best is still yet to come. Words cannot fully express how lucky, blessed and grateful I am.

TABLE OF CONTENTS

INTRODUCTION 3

Part One
RENT KILLS SMALL BUSINESSES

    Chapter 1   Why Small Businesses Fake It 13

    Chapter 2   How Small Businesses Fake It 27

Part Two
TURN THE TABLES & KILL THE RENT

    Chapter 3   What Is Serviced Office Space? 41

    Chapter 4   The Benefits of SOS 47

    Chapter 5   The Challenges with SOS 61

Part Three
KILLING THE RENT MADE EASY

    Chapter 6   Applying The 3 C's™ 67

    Chapter 7   Five Simple Steps 75

Part Four
HOW OTHERS HAVE KILLED THE RENT

How Others Have Killed The Rent 83

The Case of the Augmenting Agent 83

The Case of the Taxed Accountant 87

The Case of the Agile Attorneys 91

The Case of the Curtailing Company 95

Now Go . . . Kill The Rent & Grow Your Biz! 99

About The Author 105

References 109

"What motivates me and what keeps me coming in through the bumps and lumps that come along with being a business owner is knowing that I'm really helping other business owners achieve their goals, and we're on this journey together."
~L.D. Howard

INTRODUCTION

Fake it 'til you make it.

That's an adage most of us have heard — perhaps even lived by — at some point in our lives.

And if you're like many of the people I've met — even myself at one point — you're faking it with your small business.

How Are You Faking It?

You might be faking it by working out of your home. Like many small-business owners, you rationalize — "I have everything I need right here at home to run my business just like a pro: a dedicated space with a desk, computer, printer, telephone, file cabinets and even a fax machine. Everything I'd have in a 'real' office without having to pay office rent. Plus, I don't have to spend time commuting or even get out of my pajamas if I don't want to!"

You also might be faking it by using a P.O. Box as your business address — rationalizing, "I might work out of my home instead of a 'real' office, but I know it would be wise to have a separate address for my business mail, so I'll get a box at the post office."

It could be that you're faking it by conducting business at public venues — working and meeting clients at trendy coffee shops or libraries. You rationalize, "Sure, it's not a 'real' office, but at least I'm not meeting people in my house."

You might be thinking, "Where do I get the gall to tell you you're faking it?"

It's quite simple; I faked it too! When I had a small consulting business, I faked it by using a P.O. Box and working out of a spare bedroom that I used as my home office. And when I got fed up with the distractions and boredom of being at home most of the time, I upgraded to working out of the public library up the street.

Why Are You Faking It?

It costs money to start a new business, and office rent is not cheap. In fact, rent is often the most significant non-payroll expense that many businesses — of any size — have. Not to mention the additional costs of running an office, such as furnishing the space, hooking up telephones, connecting internet service, purchasing office supplies and equipment . . . the list can go on and on.

But where is the money going to come from? Investors are not flocking to your door to write you a big check, and banks don't lend to small businesses as generously as they once did. In fact, "multiple sources document a long-term decline in bank lending to small businesses in the aftermath of the 2008 economic recession"[i] which "has yet to return to pre-crisis levels."[ii]

This leaves blowing through your personal savings, maxing out your credit cards, borrowing money, or perhaps even taking out a second mortgage on your home among the limited financial options to get your business — your dream — off the ground.

This is an even scarier proposition when you consider that small businesses have a greater chance of failing in the first few years than they do in succeeding. It's true, about 22% of small businesses fail within the first year, approximately 40% fail by the third year, and less than half (48%) find a way to survive beyond five years.[iii] More often than not, in one way or another, this grim reality comes back to one thing: money — or lack thereof.

So, I get it. Small-business owners need to operate lean and avoid being killed by rent and related costs, so they do what they must — they fake it 'til they make it.

There's Got to Be a Better Way!

I admit, when I was faking it, I felt I was making a smart decision for my business. But what I soon realized is that while faking it seemed to save me money, it was actually costing me something — perceived professionalism and credibility as a business owner.

Just think about it — would you blame a prospect for politely declining the invitation for a consultation when they realize you want to meet them at a coffee shop where there is no privacy? Do you really think your customers would prefer to discuss business in your home or at a public library where there are distractions and others could overhear sensitive information, versus an office or conference room in a more professional and private setting? And do you know that some organizations will disqualify you from being able to do business with them simply because you use a P.O. Box as your company address? I'm confident that your answer to at least one — if not all — of these questions is "No," which means your faking it is costing you and your small business — and you may not even know it!

But what if there were a better way you could run your small business and still have a professional image, work in a "real" office space with a "real" address, save a significant amount of money on basic office expenses, and attract more clients versus scaring them away? What if there were a way that, instead of your small business being killed by rent, you could kill the rent?

Well, there is — *Serviced Office Space*! And believe it or not, I frequently meet small-business owners who aren't aware that this solution exists, even though it has been around for decades.

I'll tell you more about Serviced Office Space as you continue reading, but I can assure you that it can help your business.

"How?" you might ask.

For starters, I have been a user of Serviced Office Space. As I mentioned earlier, when I was working out of my home, I found myself distracted, and sometimes even bored, with the same routine and scenery day in and day out,

> I knew that regardless of how knowledgeable I was, my level of perceived credibility was lowered simply because of where I was working.

so I then began working out of the public library to have a separate place to work while avoiding the expense of office rent. Though this seemed to be working (at least in my mind) for a while, I quickly realized that a library was not the best environment to conduct business if I wanted to be taken seriously and attract clients.

I also knew that regardless of how knowledgeable I was, my level of perceived credibility was lowered simply because of where I was working. Like it or not, perception is often reality in the minds of many, including your prospective customers. But when I started using Serviced Office Space, it provided a more professional image and helped me to take myself and my business more seriously. It made me feel "corporate." And it also felt good to say to prospects "Let's meet at my office" instead of "Let's meet at the corner bakery at 3:00 p.m.!"

Secondly, as a licensed commercial real estate agent, I understand the costs and risks that come along with securing traditional commercial office space that simply do not exist with Serviced Office Space. For example, unlike traditional commercial office space where you are locked in to a fixed level of service for a fixed period of time, you have far more control over how much service you use with Serviced Office Space, as well as how long you use it and how much you'll pay.

If you're not convinced yet, I also own a Serviced Office Space business. That's right — I was so intrigued by the benefits I experienced as a user of Serviced Office Space that I opened my own Serviced Office Space business, Howard Corporate Centre, LLC, in 2012 to help other small-business owners. And during these past six years of owning and operating the business, it's been amazing to see how my clients have reaped the benefits of a professional image, significantly reduced overhead, more control over their expenses, and an improved bottom line.

But don't take my word for it — my clients have said it themselves. In an article highlighting my business, my clients shared how we helped their business grow. One client hailed the flexibility of the space, and how it is "an ideal place for small businesses to start up." And another client said that our solutions simply "make a lot of sense . . . if [he] was to start a [traditional] office, [he] would have to spend a minimum of $15,000 versus paying [substantially less] a month."[iv]

Without a doubt, it has been a privilege to help these and other small-business owners to kill the rent and grow their business — and I want to help *you*, too!

How This Book Is Organized

Kill The Rent – Grow Your Biz is written to be a conversation showing how you can begin reaping the benefits of Serviced Office Space and start improving your small business's bottom line right away.

The first part, *Rent Kills Small Businesses*, continues the discussion on how and why small businesses fake it as well as the challenges of traditional commercial office space. The next part, *Turn The Tables & Kill The Rent*, further introduces Serviced Office Space as a solution for killing the rent, as well as its benefits and challenges. The third part, *Killing The Rent Made Easy*, provides five simple steps on how you can begin benefiting from Serviced Office Space, along with an evaluative tool to guide you in doing so. The final part of the book, *How Others Have Killed The Rent*, provides real-world case studies of how Serviced Office Space has helped other business owners kill the rent, attract clients, and grow their business — and how you can, too.

I am excited to begin this journey with you, but before we continue, I want to remind you that your business — and more importantly, your dream — deserves to succeed and you need not experience another day of potentially losing clients because you're faking it. Decide now to increase the perceived credibility of your business and yourself. Decide now to kill the rent, attract more clients, and grow your business today.

Are you ready to get started? So am I — let's go!

PART ONE

RENT KILLS SMALL BUSINESSES

"Too many of us are not living our dreams because we are living our fears."
~Les Brown

CHAPTER 1

WHY SMALL BUSINESSES FAKE IT

By now, you've hopefully come to terms with the fact that you've possibly been faking it in your small business — but more importantly, that you're not alone in doing so, and there is a better way.

But before getting into the specifics of how Serviced Office Space can help small businesses kill the rent, we need to first explore why small businesses are important and the circumstances that contribute to why rent kills them in the first place.

Why Small Businesses Are Important

The U.S. Small Business Administration (SBA) defines a small business as "a business (corporate, limited liability company, or proprietorship) with 500 employees or less."[v] Within this definition, according to the SBA, are "microbusinesses" (companies with less than ten employees).[vi] "According to federal government data, there are over 7 million small businesses . . . [and] almost 80 percent of them have ten or fewer employees."[vii] In other words, most of the small businesses out there are "microbusinesses."

This is *good* news! For starters, small businesses are the engine that drive the American economy. Specifically, "small businesses account for about 99 percent of all businesses in the United States, employ about 54 percent of workers, and generate 52 percent of the gross domestic product."[viii] Quite frankly, if it were not for small businesses, the American economy would simply collapse. But more important than their economic contributions, at least in my view, small businesses are led by people who dare to pursue their *dreams*! They take risks, refuse to live a status quo life, and realize that the risk of the business failing pales in comparison to the risk of not trying, of regret, of wondering "what if?"

> According to federal government data, there are over 7 million small businesses . . . [and] almost 80 percent of them have ten or fewer employees. In other words, most of the small businesses out there are "microbusinesses."

This, greater than any of the other joys that come along with being a Serviced Office Space provider, is what warms my heart the most: seeing other business owners pursue their dreams, and being a catalyst — if only in a small way — to help them succeed in doing so.

The Money Dilemma

But despite their importance to the economy, many small businesses face a money dilemma. In fact, 82% of small businesses that fail do so because of cash flow problems.[ix] But the options and likelihood of securing funding to start or expand a small business can be limited . . . and risky.

> 82% of businesses that fail do so because of cash flow problems.

Certainly, there are a number of books and other resources that take a deeper dive into options for financing your business, and I strongly encourage you to explore those resources to determine what options are best for you. But below is a very brief overview of some of the money challenges small businesses might encounter.

SBA/Bank Loans

The first place a new small business may go for funding is the SBA, whose loans are government-backed and provided to small businesses through banks and other lenders, including credit unions. The SBA does not lend directly to small-business owners, rather it provides loan *guarantees* to businesses, promising banks to pay back a certain percentage of a loan if the borrower is unable to.[x]

Although the SBA has a variety of lending programs designed specifically for the needs of small businesses and there are express application options, most of the loans require a great deal of paperwork, and the time it takes to complete the required materials and obtain approval can take 60–90 days, perhaps even longer. You should also note that a personal guaranty will be required for anyone who owns 20% or more of the business, which may require your personal assets to be used as collateral if your business assets are not sufficient.

So, for a small-business owner who needs cash relatively quickly or who does not want to put their personal assets at risk, an SBA loan may not be a good fit.

Investors
Another funding source that you might consider for your small business is an investor. Keep in mind, though, that investors are typically only interested in businesses "offering the prospect of long-term capital gains sizable enough to offset the short-term risks and illiquidity. [S]mall businesses with annual growth rates projected below 20 percent are of little interest to outside investors."[xi]

But even if you do attract the interest of an investor, they will likely want a share of your business (equity) and will want to be paid back—with a significant return on their investment. Beyond that, depending upon how the investment agreement is structured, the investor might also have a say in business decisions, and you may have to report the arrangement to the Securities Exchange Commission. According to one source, working with an investor should involve "the guidance of an experienced and knowledgeable securities attorney . . . [and] you should expect to spend at least $15,000 in fees."[xii]

Business Grants

Another funding option for your small business may be grants, which can be provided by governmental agencies, private sector corporations, or non-profit organizations. The amount of the grant can vary widely depending upon grantor, but you can typically expect the process of researching and applying for a

> Some grants are not necessarily free money, and usually require the recipient to match funds or combine the grant with other forms of financing such as a loan.

grant that fits your business needs to be cumbersome and lengthy. You should also keep in mind that the "SBA does NOT provide grants for starting and expanding a business . . . [and some grants] are not necessarily free money, and usually require the recipient to match funds or combine the grant with other forms of financing, such as a loan."[xiii]

Crowdfunding

"Crowdfunding denotes the pooling of capital from multiple retail investors. Peer-to-peer lending is a form of crowdfunding in which an individual borrower receives a personal loan."[xiv] Although crowdfunding may create an easier way for some small businesses to generate funds for their business, it does come with risks, one of which is "the chance of having your product or idea ripped off. . . Trademarks and patents do provide some defensibility, but they are hard to enforce internationally."[xv]

> Trademarks and patents . . . are hard to enforce internationally.

Factoring

Another financing option that some small businesses sometimes use is factoring, an arrangement in which "a company uses its accounts receivables [money coming in] to raise cash. But rather than using receivables as collateral for a loan, the company actually sells its accounts receivable to a finance company, known as the factor."[xvi] Keep in mind, however, that "the factor does not pay the company 100 cents on the dollar [and] there are also charges and commissions for its collection services."[xvii]

Additionally, factoring can be risky because the receivables that are being factored (and for which you are receiving monies in advance) may not come to fruition (e.g., you might have a client that defaults on an agreement for which your factor has advanced to you a portion of the full contract value), which may require you to pay money back to your factor and cost you even more.

Personal Resources

If no other financing options are viable for you, all that may be left is using your personal financial resources. Sometimes referred to as *bootstrapping* — "a means of financing a small [business] . . . without raising equity from traditional sources or borrowing money from a bank (Freear, Sohl, and Wetzel, 1995b)"[xviii] — using personal resources to finance your business includes "personal credit cards, loans from family and friends, and home equity loans" [xix] with "the most common source of capital to finance business expansion [being] personal and family savings."[xx]

Using personal funds is a common way to finance a new small business. In fact, in a 2012 survey of business owners, it was found that an overwhelming number of small businesses (57%) use personal savings for startup capital for their business.[xxi]

> 57% of small businesses use personal savings for startup capital for their business.

There is a benefit to using your own personal funds — if you put your own money into financing your business, it shows that you've got "skin in the game." This could help if you decide to apply for a loan later because it shows prospective lenders that you're serious about your business and that you're willing to share some — if not most — of the financial risk to do so. Just think about it — why would a bank lend you money when you haven't invested anything into your business yourself?

But using personal funds also has risks. For example, if you're considering using personal credit cards to finance your business, which an average of 8% of small businesses do,[xxii] keep in mind that credit card interest rates can be ridiculously high, about 13%[xxiii] or potentially more than double that rate if your credit is challenged. High credit card usage can also adversely impact your credit score, reducing the likelihood of getting an SBA or other loan later. Also, borrowing money from family and friends can strain relationships, and taking out a second mortgage can potentially jeopardize your home if you aren't able to repay the debt.

A Common Response to the Money Dilemma
So, if small businesses have limited (and risky) options to finance their business, and will likely have to wait at least a few years before the business is generating enough income to sustain itself, what is the alternative? Asked a different way, if a small-business owner can't immediately increase the money coming in, they have to decrease the money going out, right?

And what's the easiest way to do that? *They fake it!*

Commercial Office Rent Isn't Cheap

In an ideal world, you'll have more than sufficient money to easily afford professional office space for your small business. But as we've discussed, there may be challenges you'll encounter in securing those funds to do so. And even if you are able to secure funds for your office space, my experience and observations as a licensed commercial real estate agent reveal other obstacles you may face:

- Some landlords won't even lease space to you as a new or small business because of the inherent risk (i.e., high default rate, no long-term track record of success).
- Of the landlords who are willing to take a chance on you, they might require you to pay a higher security deposit (e.g., three months or more) and sign a "personal guaranty" — which effectively means that if your business fails, the business can no longer pay rent, or you otherwise default, the landlord can sue the guarantor of the lease (typically the business owner) for any unpaid rent, including going after the guarantor's personal assets to do so.
- Landlords typically want prospective tenants to commit to a lease term of at least three years.

- Most rent will escalate (increase) each year, typically by at least three percent.
- If you find a space that you like, don't expect to be able to move in right away. Even if you are moving into a space "as-is," it takes time to negotiate and agree to lease terms, for an attorney (yours and the landlord's) to review the lease, and to fulfill any governmental requirements (e.g., permits). Instead, expect to wait at least a minimum of 60 days (or even longer if you are planning to make modifications to the space).

Couple all of the above with the fact that there may simply be a limited inventory of office space that will meet your business's needs — or its budget.

To illustrate, I once had a prospective real estate client who wanted to secure a 750 square foot commercial office space for her new business. The maximum she wanted to pay for rent was $800 per month.

Unfortunately for the prospect, there simply were no spaces that small available for lease in the geographical area she was interested in. Even if there was, the typical price per square foot in her desired area was about $19 (on the low end), so a budget of $800 for rent was simply not realistic, as shown:

Commercial Office Rent (Idealistic)

750 per square feet
x $19 per square foot
= $14,250 per year
= $1,187 per month

Of course, space inventory and costs per square foot vary by region and space type, and there are other factors that impact what your final monthly rent payment will be. But assuming a minimum commercial office space of 1,000 square feet and a minimum cost per square foot of $19, you would need a budget of nearly $1,600 per month just to cover rent in the first year as shown (and remember, as I noted earlier, lease amounts typically increase each year).

Commercial Office Rent (More Realistic)

1,000 per square feet
x $19 per square foot
= $19,000 per year
= $1,583 per month

This, of course, is in addition to the costs of buying furniture and other expenses associated with leasing traditional commercial office space.

***

Though the money dilemma and the high costs of traditional commercial office space are two key reasons why small businesses fake it, the good news is that Serviced Office Space resolves both of these issues, as you'll learn later in the book.

What's even better is that you don't have to wait 60 days (or longer) to begin using Serviced Office Space; it's a solution that you can put into action today!

Ready to learn more? Of course you are, so turn the page!

Key Points:

- Office rent is often the most significant non-payroll operating expense for businesses of any size.
- The reason small businesses fake it is twofold: the money dilemma and the high cost of traditional commercial office space.

Action Exercises:

1. Research financing options for your business, including:
    - The amount of funding you are likely to receive
    - The length of time that it would likely take for you to receive the funding

- The interest rate and amount of time that you would have to repay, if applicable

A good place to start this research is with a local small business banker.

2. Research the costs of traditional commercial office space in your area.
    - For example, how much would it cost to lease a 1,000 square foot office space per year?

A good place to start this research is www.loopnet.com.

CHAPTER 2

HOW SMALL BUSINESSES FAKE IT

In the last chapter, we further explored two key reasons why small businesses fake it; so this leads us to the discussion of *how* small businesses fake it.

For many new small-business owners, faking it entails working out of their home. This may seem to make sense, especially if you're a "solopreneur." I mean, you don't have to go far to get to your "office," and if you're like me, when I worked out of my home, sometimes you might not even leave your bed!

But what about when it's time to meet with prospects? Will they mind coming to your house? Will they question your legitimacy as a business person for not having a "real" office? Conversely, will you feel safe, having someone in your house you might have never met before?

And what if your meeting with the prospect is interrupted by your dog barking — even worse, what if your prospect doesn't like your dog? Do you think the prospect will really want to do business with you, or chose you over another business with a nice office in a professional building?

Let's be honest. If the tables were turned, and you had to decide between doing business with a company operating in a professional setting versus one operating out of a home office or public venue, which one would you be more impressed by? Which one would you choose to do business with?

Dining Room a.k.a. Corporate Headquarters
Or, let's imagine you have dedicated a day to work on a proposal that will open so many doors for your business. The proposal is due today, so you've decided not to schedule any meetings. You're just going to focus on getting the proposal done, and you have even cleared off the dining room table so you have plenty of room to organize your paperwork.

About two hours in, you remember that your "power suit" is at the dry cleaners and you need it for a major meeting tomorrow. You simply will not survive the meeting without your suit, and need to get to the cleaners before too much of the day gets away from you. You decide to take a quick break from working on the proposal and drive to the cleaners. You tell yourself, "It's right around the corner, so it will only take a second, and it will break the monotony of being in the house all day."

When you arrive at the cleaners, you make small talk with the owner as she's getting your suit. You've been a patron of her store for years, and you always enjoy talking and catching up with her. As she's ringing you up, one of your neighbors comes in and the two of you begin talking and catching up, too. After a while, you realize you need to get going, so you say your goodbyes and head out of the dry cleaners with your "power suit" in tow.

As you're pulling out of the parking lot, you remember that a grocery store is nearby, so you decide to make a quick stop to pick up some household goods and other items for dinner tonight. You tell yourself, "It will save me from having to run out later on, and it will only take a second." While in the grocery store, you quickly find everything you're looking for — and some of the items are even on sale! — but the lines are a little longer than you expected this time of day, so you wind up spending more time than anticipated on your impromptu shopping spree. But you don't fret — the lines are moving relatively quickly and you still have plenty of time to finish working on your proposal.

When you eventually make it home, you decide to quickly turn on the news to see what the major headlines are. You tell yourself, "I need to let my head air out a few more minutes before resuming work on the proposal — my brain is still a little fried from working on it so long earlier." You flip through the channels and come across some folks talking about a story that's been trending in the news. The issue does not impact you or anyone you know, but you're emotionally invested in it and must remain up to date with what's happening.

In fact, you post about it on social media because it's important that your connections know your opinion on the matter and that you're in the know, even though they likely just saw the same headlines you did. Within seconds of making your post, you get many comments, likes and shares (what an ego boost!), and you decide to respond to all of them right away — I mean, it would be rude if you didn't, right? You wind up having an interesting "dialogue" about the news issue via social media, but after a while you decide it's time to get back to work.

By the time you finally resume working on your proposal, you realize that a significant amount of time has passed since deciding to go to the dry cleaners and you now don't have nearly as much time as you would have liked to have to submit a quality proposal by today's deadline (but you would have had plenty of time if you didn't go to the dry cleaners . . . watch television . . . post on social media . . . you get the drift).

So now you're rushing. Somehow, you submit the proposal on time but it's not the quality you intended it to be. There was additional information that you would have liked to incorporate, but because you didn't allot the time to properly research and gather information, you didn't include it.

> It is easy to get distracted when you work out of your home, which can amount to precious time being lost in moving your business forward.

A few weeks later, you learn your proposal wasn't selected. When you inquire, you're told that the selected proposal included information that you intended to include in yours but didn't — because you chose to do other things that you convinced yourself would "only take a second."

This is what a "free" home office can cost you.

As you can see (and may have already experienced), it is easy to get distracted when you work out of your home, and you will be amazed by how quickly "a second" or a "quick break" can amount to precious time being lost in moving your business forward.

Besides the commonly known distractions, there are other disadvantages to conducting business out of your home. For starters, zoning regulations may restrict or prohibit commercial activities in a residential property, and there may be restrictions in your lease or homeowner's association covenants.

There are also liability issues to consider when running a business out of your home. For instance, according to the National Association of Small Business's 2015 Economic Report, the majority of small businesses surveyed are S-corporations (42%), followed by LLCs (23%).[xxiv] LLCs and corporations should think twice about using a home address for a small business. One of the major benefits of these business structures is limited liability for business debts and activities. However, this protection only applies if you keep your business and personal activities separate. Using a personal address for a business could pierce the corporate veil, making you personally liable for business debts and obligations.[xxv]

> Using a personal address for a business could pierce the corporate veil, making you personally liable for business debts and obligations.

BONUS POINTS!
Check your renters' or homeowners' insurance to see what, if any, coverages are included for claims arising out of your operating a business from your home.

Corporate Contract vs. Coffee & Croissant

"Okay," you say, "I get it. I won't work in my home; too many distractions." Instead, you decide to work out of the corner coffee shop. You can get a good cup of joe, a fresh pastry, and you'll break the monotony of working out of your home all day.

So, when a prospect recently called to express interest in your services, you asked him to meet you at the coffee shop. It's a very popular spot and you're sure your prospect would like the environment — everybody in the neighborhood does. Plus, they have a five-star rating online and a "cool vibe," so you decide it will be a perfect place for a business meeting.

You arrive at the coffee shop a little early (I mean, you are a professional), and while you are waiting, you order coffee and a pastry — which costs you about $9. You take a seat in the rear of the shop, which is a little quieter, and settle in a spot by a large window with a nice view of the shop's parking lot.

A few sips into your coffee and bites into your pastry, your prospect arrives. You see him looking around aimlessly in the lobby for you, so you leave your window seat in the rear (leaving your coffee, pastry, computer, and other materials unattended) to escort him back. You warmly greet each other by shaking hands, and since you're in the lobby, you ask him if he wants anything to eat. You know that it takes money to make money, so you don't mind spending another $9 to help seal the deal.

Once you and your prospect are settled back in the rear seating area, you begin talking and learning more about his needs and how your company can help him. During the pitch, you attempt to show the prospect a chart that you spent hours preparing last night, but you're not able to pull it up as quickly as you'd like because the shop's open internet is a little slow. But after a few minutes, the document finally opens.

You feel really good about how the meeting is going. Your prospect seems interested and is asking some good questions. Just when you feel ready to go in for the close, a family of five enters the shop and sits in the area right beside where you and your prospect are meeting.

The family appears to be on vacation, with a mom, dad, teenager, toddler, and infant. They're excitedly talking about their plans for the day, and laughing about how much fun they had last night. Because it's a little early in

CHAPTER 2: HOW SMALL BUSINESSES FAKE IT 35

the morning, the baby is a little fussy, crying quite a bit, though the parents do their best to quiet the baby down.

You continue with your presentation, but now it's difficult for you and your prospect to hear each other. More importantly, because you're now about to talk about sensitive, financial issues, your prospect expresses concern about continuing the meeting where others can hear, and suggests continuing the meeting later in the week via a conference call.

Though you would prefer to finish and close the deal now, you respectfully agree with the prospect's suggestion and schedule a time to talk later in the week. You escort your prospect as he leaves the coffee shop (again, leaving your belongings unattended) and return to the seating area to collect your things, smiling at the family as you exit.

You feel bummed. You were expecting to close this deal today, and now you won't even speak to the prospect again until later in the week. You know that this interruption has cost you a loss in momentum, and possibly the deal.

When you return home, you reflect on what happened at the coffee shop and how it could have gone better. You thought you did everything right — you scheduled the meeting in the morning, when the shop is usually quiet, and sat at a spot in the rear, where there is usually less patron traffic.

You weren't expecting a family to come in and sit right next to you, and it certainly never occurred to you that your prospect would cut the meeting short as a result. You thought your prospect would like meeting at a popular coffee shop and sitting in a nice, quiet booth in the rear with a large window — but maybe he didn't.

Because you're wiser from today's experience, you have a fleeting thought about conducting future business meetings at the public library instead, but you realize that you could possibly run into some issues there, too. Sure, the library has private meeting rooms you can rent, but they require you to reserve (and pay for) at least a two-hour block, even though your meetings typically last an hour or less. You don't want to pay for time you don't need, and the library won't allow you to bring food or beverages on site, so no coffee and pastries for you or your prospects.

You've learned — very painfully — that options for conducting business that you thought were "free" — working at home or at a public venue — can actually cost you a lot. You also know that the idea of signing a three-year lease (and paying hundreds or thousands of dollars a month for rent) for a traditional commercial office space is also not a viable option at this stage in your business.

So what are you to do? How can you have a place to conduct business that won't scare off your current and prospective clients and won't break your bank?

It's simple — Serviced Office Space!

Key Points:

- In addition to the distractions you will likely encounter, conducting business out of your home may be restricted by zoning regulations, lease terms, and/or homeowners' association covenants.
- Privacy issues are among the challenges you'll face when working at public venues, like coffee shops and libraries.

Action Exercises:

1. Research the zoning regulations in your area for any restrictions and/or prohibitions for operating a business out of your home.
2. Review your lease or homeowners' association covenants for restrictions in operating a business out of your home.

PART TWO

TURN THE TABLES & KILL THE RENT

*"A problem is a chance for you
to do your best."
~Duke Ellington*

CHAPTER 3

WHAT IS SERVICED OFFICE SPACE?

By now, I know you're probably eager to learn more about how Serviced Office Space can help your business. The obvious first question is "What is Serviced Office Space?"

In simple terms, Serviced Office Space (SOS) is an alternative to a traditional commercial office, enabling you to have access to a professional setting for as little or as long as you want. If you need a place to conduct a meeting for just an hour — you can do just that. If you need to use the space for longer, well, you can do that, too!

And unlike working out of your home or a public venue, SOS offers an environment in which you will be perceived as more professional and credible, leaving a far more positive impression. When you opt for SOS, your prospects will be warmly greeted by a professional staff person — not your dog (no offense to your fur baby)!

In short, what this ultimately means is that you have much more control over when and how often you use the space — no three-year lease required. And many of the costs that would come along with establishing your own traditional commercial office are eliminated because they are included with SOS — so you're not only "killing" your rent but also cutting many of the ancillary costs of having an office, too.

There are many names for SOS, including but not limited to:

- Business Service Center
- Fractional Workspace
- Hot Desk
- Incubator
- Shared Workspace
- Virtual Office

Though the names vary, they all refer to a way in which a professional office or workspace can be provided and used on demand.

And the reality is that the on-demand nature of SOS is in line with the way people are working and want to receive their products and services nowadays. People don't want to wait anymore; they like to have transportation with a few clicks of a mouse or taps on an app — hence the many ridesharing options that are now available. And many people prefer to shop from the convenience of their computer or mobile device versus driving to a mall — hence the increase in online shopping. Well, you can also have a professional office space on demand, too!

To help further explain SOS, I'll summarize it into two categories: Executive Suites and Coworking.

Executive Suites

Executive Suites are a more formal, structured SOS option, typically a suite of separate, private offices and meeting rooms. This particular variation of SOS is designed more for those who enjoy working independently, and may be more appealing to lawyers, accountants and other professionals preferring a more autonomous work environment. Though I often encounter business people who are not aware of Executive Suites, the model actually dates back several decades.

Coworking

"Coworking, a type of shared workplace, is an emerging model which provides many of the amenities of traditional serviced offices but places a much greater emphasis on designing a space that creates a community and an experience for users."[xxvi] Coworking has become a more popular form of SOS in recent years, but the concept can be traced back as far as 15th century Florence, when "[b]ottega workshops brought together different types of talent to compete, collaborate, learn and improve. These bottegas created environments that increased the level of discussion among diverse groups and helped these individuals to turn their ideas into actions. The interactions led to higher levels of innovation for all."[xxvii]

Unlike Executive Suites, Coworking models tend to have more open floor plans, and may be more attractive to those who enjoy working in a collaborative, communal environment.

Hybrid Model
To satisfy the needs of both work styles — the independent worker and the collaborative worker — some SOS providers offer a hybrid model that includes private offices as well as Coworking areas for collaborative interaction, such as lounges and team areas. Even some coffee shops have added (or morphed into) Coworking venues to benefit from the growing trend.[xxviii]

The types of workspaces available with SOS are as diverse as the names that refer to it. They can vary from a single, open desk to a 20-seat conference room. Or even from a small private office to a large meeting room that can accommodate 50 or more people. The options are practically endless, and you have the control to decide what best suits your needs — and budget.

***

But despite all of the different types of SOS and the flexibility it offers, what is particularly interesting to me is that in my six years as a SOS provider, there are many business owners who are simply not aware of the options available to them.

But now *you* know that you can have a professional environment to operate your business without paying for office rent and other costs associated with leasing a traditional commercial office space (assuming a landlord will even take a risk on you in the first place).

You also now know that you don't have to make a long-term commitment or pay for more office space than you need, and you no longer have to lose prospects or miss opportunities just because you work out of your home or in a public venue. Instead, you'll impress and attract more clients because you're working in a professional setting with many of the features and amenities that typically accompany traditional commercial office spaces, but at a fraction of the cost.

The ways that SOS can help you cut costs, attract clients, and improve your bottom line are almost endless, so let's further explore some of the benefits of SOS in the next chapter.

Are you excited yet? Great — I am, too!

Key Points:

- SOS is an alternative to traditional commercial office space.
- There are two basic categories of SOS: Executive Suites and Coworking. Executive Suites are a more formal model of SOS whereas Coworking is a more collaborative, communal model of SOS.
- Though SOS is referenced by many names, they all refer to a form of on-demand office space.

Action Exercises:

1. Have you ever heard of SOS or any of the names often used to refer to it?
2. Conduct an internet search of SOS in your area and see what you find.

CHAPTER 4

THE BENEFITS OF SOS

In just a few chapters, we've covered quite a bit, including two key challenges facing many small businesses, and how SOS is a solution.

Now, let's talk more about some of the specific benefits of using SOS.

The 3 C's™
I have developed a guide to help business owners evaluate prospective SOS providers. The guide, called *The 3 C's of Serviced Office Space*™ or simply *"The 3 C's*™*,"* provides three dimensions for evaluating SOS: *Credibility, Convenience,* and *Control.*

Credibility: As we've talked about earlier, the idea of conducting a business meeting in your home or a public venue leaves a different — and lesser — impression than working in a professional environment. Like it or not, perception is reality, and operating your business out of an office in a professional setting creates a far greater perception of credibility than working at a coffee shop or library. So, when you think of credibility, think of the extent to which SOS will improve your professional image and perception as a legitimate business owner.

Convenience: This dimension is two-fold; it pertains to the SOS location and ease of access to services. I know you're probably thinking, "But working out of my home *is* a convenient location for me!" This might be true, or at least it might seem true — but what about missed opportunities that come along with doing so — is that a convenience, too? In my view, a convenient location is not so much to benefit you but rather your prospects and clients — the location must be convenient and accessible for *them* so *they* can easily purchase your product and/or service.

In addition, it should be convenient for you to access the SOS provider's services — from how your mail is handled, to how you reserve an office or meeting room, and everything in between. Accessing the SOS provider's services should be seamless and efficient, enabling you to focus on what you want to do most — grow your business.

> The 3 C's of Serviced Office Space™ are credibility, convenience, and control.

Control: With SOS, you decide how much or how little of the services you will use. If you only need to use a space for an hour, well, that's what you'll do. If you don't want to enter into a long-term agreement, you don't have to! SOS is based on *your* needs; you should always feel that you are in control when it comes to your chosen selection. You should never feel like you have to use more of the service than you feel you need.

Cost Savings vs. Traditional Commercial Office Space

As you learned earlier, you can expect to have a great deal of up-front costs to operate your business from a traditional commercial office space. Not only the security deposits and fees required by governmental entities, but also costs to furnish the office, purchase equipment and office supplies, hire an assistant or a receptionist—the list goes on.

But with SOS, not only do the costs of starting the service pale in comparison to that of a traditional commercial office space, but many of the other costs are also included with the service. The following chart illustrates some of the cost savings you can realize with SOS.

TRADITIONAL COMMERCIAL OFFICE SPACE VS. SOS

	Traditional Commercial Office Space	SOS
Office Space Rental	600 sf @ $19 per sf Includes private office, reception area, kitchenette, and conference room	Full time use of private office, including reception area, conference room, and kitchen access
Monthly Office Space	**$950**	**$800**
Furniture Leases	Private Office: Desk, executive chair, two guest chairs, and lateral file Reception Area: Reception desk and chair, four guest seats Conference Room: Conference room table, eight chairs	Included
Monthly Furniture Lease	**$600**	**N/A**
Receptionist Services	Receptionist working 20 hours per week at $15/hour + 10% for payroll taxes	Included
Monthly Receptionist Salary	**$1,320**	**N/A**
Equipment Lease	Multi-function copier/scanner/fax Filtered water dispenser	Included
Monthly Equipment Lease	**$200**	**N/A**
Telephone and Internet	Telephone lines and internet connection for office space	Typically Included *(or a nominal fee)*
Monthly Telephone & Internet	**$400**	**N/A**
Office Supplies	For Copier: paper and toner For Kitchen: cups, napkins, coffee, tea, creamer, sugar	Included
Monthly Office Supplies	**$100**	**N/A**
Office Maintenance	Utilities, janitorial services, repairs and maintenance	Included
Monthly Office Maintenance	**$400**	**N/A**
TOTAL MONTHLY COSTS	**$3,970**	**$800**
TOTAL ANNUAL COSTS	**$47,640**	**$9,600**

As shown, by killing the rent and choosing SOS, you can potentially save nearly *$40,000* a year, which can instead be invested into your business.

Faster Startup

Instead of waiting at least 60 days to occupy a traditional commercial office space, you can typically begin utilizing SOS within a few days, if not the same day. As I mentioned earlier, SOS is an on-demand service, so it is available to you when you need it.

Physical Street Address

With SOS, you will have a "real" street address for your business — not a P.O. Box. And, unlike some other services that claim to provide a street address, with SOS, photos of an actual office building will appear when the address is researched on the internet. On the same note, should a visitor stop by your office unannounced, they'll walk into an actual office environment (versus a strip mall).

Professional Image

As stated before, having a real, physical address lends itself to a more professional image and higher credibility. Further, when your guests are greeted by a receptionist and conduct their business with you in a private office or meeting room, they can't help but be impressed!

Secured & Faster Internet

Unlike most public venues that typically have open (unsecured) internet networks, SOS operators typically provide internet access that is secured and password-protected and with faster speeds (so no need to worry about slow file loads like you experienced at the corner coffee shop).

Secured Premises

Travel back in time with me to the coffee shop where you met your prospect (and the family of five). Remember when you left your belongings unattended to initially greet your prospect and then again when you walked him out after the meeting ended? You took a big risk in doing this — someone could have easily taken your belongings in that short period of time, and we can only image the plethora of other problems that would have followed.

Fortunately, with SOS, you can choose to work from a private office or meeting room in which you can keep your belongings secured at all times. If you need to step away from your workspace to meet someone in the lobby, grab something to eat, or for some other purpose, there are staff onsite to ensure your belongings are not disrupted, and you may even have the ability to lock the workspace until you return.

Use As You Go

As I've said before, SOS is an on-demand service, so you can use as little of the services as you need and want, and scale as your business grows.

Kitchen Access

SOS providers typically offer kitchen access, including coffee, tea, water, and a microwave and refrigerator. While you're using the space, you'll be able to keep yourself hydrated and can save money by packing your breakfast and/or lunch and nuking it in the microwave!

And the coffee and pastries most likely will be free for you and your guests. This may not seem significant on its surface, but you will be surprised how much money this can save you versus working out of a public venue.

For example, going back to the neighborhood coffee shop, remember when you paid $9 for a cup of coffee and croissant? Well, imagine that you did this three times a week, and each time you also treated your guest to the same (with you being a big spender and wanting to impress a potential new client)!

You'd be spending *over $200* a month alone just for coffee and croissants:

The Cost of Coffee & Croissants

18 Coffee and croissant for you & your guest
x 3 times per week
= $54 per week
= $216 per month

No Build-Out

Unlike traditional commercial office space where you may have to wait (and possibly pay) for certain areas of the space to be modified for your specific needs, SOS typically has ready-made offices and meeting rooms just waiting for your use.

Signage
Should you opt to use an office with an SOS provider on a full-time basis, you may have signage on or near the office door - which further promotes a corporate image and helps to convey that it is "your" office. You may also be able to have your company listed on a building directory.

Access to Resources
In addition to furniture typically being included with SOS, you will also have access to the provider's equipment, such as a copy machine, scanner, and projector. You can also typically have access to the provider's staff for administrative support for a lesser cost than hiring your own staff person.

A "Greener" Way to Work
Utilizing SOS is a way to reduce your carbon footprint. For example, instead of occupying a 1,000-square foot space which you may not fully utilize, you can use an office or meeting room just as you need it. Furthermore, "compared to utilizing a traditional office, [SOS uses] just a fraction of the resources. Thanks to the fact that an [SOS] location can be shared among numerous other

small businesses, the usage of all of the electric, water and other resources are significantly decreased."[xxix]

Psychological/Other Benefits

If the above is not enough to convince you that you have a lot to gain by using SOS, take note of some of the feedback I've received from SOS customers:

- *I like being able to get out of the house and not feeling isolated. SOS is a more professional environment where I can be more productive and interact with others.*
- *When I used my home address as my business address, prospective customers would find me on the internet and come to my home unannounced to inquire about my services. With SOS, walk-ins go to a corporate location instead, and the staff knows exactly how to handle them if I'm not available.*
- *There are so many disruptions and distractions when I work at home. I can concentrate more when I use SOS.*
- *When I work at home, I sometimes don't even get out of my pajamas. I like having a reason to dress up professionally. When I'm dressed better, I feel better; when I feel better, I do better.*
- *I like having a routine and structure outside of the house. This, along with having a professional office in a nice building, makes me feel more like a CEO.*
- *I like not having to stress about paying rent, utilities, etc. I pay one monthly amount and the SOS provider*

takes care of the rest so I can focus on growing my business.

SOS Benefits for Businesses That Are Not Faking It
In the next chapter, I'll discuss some of the challenges of SOS. But before doing so, I want to point out that while this book focuses on the benefits of SOS for small businesses that are faking it, its benefits can extend to larger businesses or those that may not necessarily be faking it.

Why is this important to know? Well, while your business may be small (and faking it) now, you may have aspirations of growing into a medium or large-sized business with access to all of the financial resources you can ever imagine. And when that time comes, SOS can still help you save money.

You might also be thinking that because a physical space is not required to operate your business, SOS cannot benefit you — but it actually could.

To be clear, I'm not one to assert that anything is a one-size-fits-all solution or a one-all-be-all for everyone. Sometimes, regardless of how great a solution is, it just may not be a fit for your needs. But I'd like to offer some illustrations of how SOS can support the needs of larger and other businesses that are not faking it — you might be surprised how SOS can help.

Online Businesses

Q: My business is 100% online. How can SOS help me?

A: Even though your business is online, "some clients may [still] steer away from businesses that provide no contact address, or only a P.O. box number—for example, people may worry that businesses without physical addresses might disappear without a trace."[xxx] You can use SOS as a professional address for your corporate headquarters, and as a professional place to meet with your team members or strategic partners when needed.

Existing Business

Q: I have been in business for several years and have my own, traditional commercial office space. What value does SOS offer me?

A: SOS can allow your business to have a presence in new demographic areas to attract more clients without having to physically be there (i.e., a satellite office). Also, if you ever decide to expand your business and open up an office in a new market, SOS can allow you to temporarily test a new market pre-expansion without having to make a long-term commitment to do so.

Governmental Entities/Large Companies

Q: Our company has had massive growth and is very large; money isn't an issue for us. I don't think SOS could ever accommodate our physical needs — could it?

A: Yes! For instance, you can use SOS as an alternate location for training sessions if your location is maxed out or if you would like to reach a different geographical market. In my SOS business, I have also had governmental entities use our space as a field office for project managers, providing them with a more professional and less expensive solution than working out of a trailer, for example.

Key Points:

- *The 3 C's of Serviced Office Space™* are convenience, credibility, and control.
- Businesses can save a significant amount of money by using SOS, which can then be invested into the business.
- SOS can support the needs of businesses of different sizes and types, including businesses that are not faking it.

Action Exercises:

1. Think about *The 3 C's of Serviced Office Space*™ as discussed in this chapter. In what way(s) are *The 3 C's*™ important to your business?
2. Based on what we've covered thus far, think of three ways that SOS can help your business.

CHAPTER 5

THE CHALLENGES WITH SOS

Clearly, there are a myriad of benefits from using SOS for your business. In my view — as a former SOS customer, a current SOS provider, and as a professional in the traditional commercial real estate industry — I believe that the benefits of SOS far outweigh any potential challenges.

But I would be remiss in not addressing some of the challenges that you might experience, too. So, in the interest of full disclosure, I'll discuss challenges that I hear most frequently from SOS users.

Sharing Space with Others

When you use SOS, it's quite possible that you'll frequently notice other customers using the space, which you may not like depending upon your preferred work style. For instance, you might be able to hear the user in a neighboring space talking on the phone, chatter from another user's training session down the hall, or activity from an event that the SOS provider is conducting.

Most SOS providers are good at keeping a pleasant environment for its users, and some even have designated "quiet areas," but just be mindful that others are using the space to grow their business, too, and sounds will carry. As you are evaluating SOS providers, you may want to inquire about their noise policy.

Desired Space Availability Not Guaranteed

If you find an SOS provider with an office that has your name written all over it or a conference room that you feel you can be most productive in — great, you've found a home for your business! Just be aware, though, that because you are competing with other users, typically on a first-come-first-served basis, you are not necessarily guaranteed to get your desired space when you want it.

By the same token, if you opt to use a full-time office, the SOS provider might not be able (or willing) to guarantee your continued use beyond your initial term.

***

Now that you have a better sense of what to expect with SOS and its benefits and challenges, how do you decide what's best for your business?

Great question! Remember *The 3 C's of Serviced Office Space*™ I discussed earlier? Well, I've created a tool to help you evaluate SOS options along these parameters and to help you make the best selection for you.

I am nearly as excited about you beginning to take this step toward advancing your business as you are — so let's get started!

Key Points:

1. There are some challenges with using SOS; however, to a large extent, the benefits outweigh the challenges.

Action Exercises:

1. Do the challenges identified in this chapter impact your decision to use SOS? Please explain.
2. What, if any, additional challenges might you face with SOS for your specific business?

PART THREE

KILLING THE RENT MADE EASY

*"Price is what you pay.
Value is what you get."*
~Warren Buffet

CHAPTER 6

APPLYING THE 3 C'S™

So, how do you decide which SOS provider is best for you? Indeed, there are many options to choose from, and you need a way to easily assess and narrow down your options (I mean, you don't want to spend too much time evaluating your options — you want to get to work, right)?

What you'll see on the next page is an evaluation grid of *The 3 C's*™ to help you to assess prospective SOS providers along the parameters I mentioned earlier: credibility, convenience, and control.

THE 3 C'S OF SERVICED OFFICE SPACE™ Evaluation Grid			
	SOS Provider #1 Name: Address: Contact Person:	SOS Provider #2 Name: Address: Contact Person:	SOS Provider #3 Name: Address: Contact Person:
Credibility *Examples:* • *Business Address* • *Professional Atmosphere & Staff* • *Lobby Listing/Signage* • *No/Low Provider Branding* • *Administrative Support Services*			
CREDIBILITY Score			
Convenience *Examples:* • *Location* • *Parking* • *Accessibility* • *Available Amenities*			
CONVENIENCE Score			
Control *Examples:* • *Diversity of Services* • *Flexible Agreement Terms* • *Ease of Use*			
CONTROL Score			
OVERALL IMPRESSION **Total Score = 15**			

Additional Notes

SOS Provider Evaluation Guide

5 = Excellent *(Translation: "This place rocks! Where do I sign?")*

4 = Very good *(Translation: "This is pretty nice")*

3 = Good *(Translation: "Not bad")*

2 = Fair *(Translation: "Meh")*

1 = Poor *(Translation: "No way – next!")*

Guide to Using *The 3 C's*™ Evaluation Grid

Now let's talk a little more about some common factors to consider under each category on *The 3 C's*™ Evaluation Grid as you're searching for an SOS provider for your business.

Credibility Factors: As I mentioned in an earlier chapter, credibility is all about improving your professionalism and image as a business person. Some guiding questions include: To what extent does this location improve my corporate image? What features does the location offer to help with this?

> Business Address: Does the location have a "real" business address that you can use as your company's address? Is the location in a nice, safe, and well-maintained building? Can I receive mail and packages here — will someone be available to sign for them? Can the location also be used as a drop-off location for clients and prospects? Can my mail be forwarded or otherwise handled as I request?

> Professional Atmosphere & Staff: Are the staff at the location professional, helpful, and friendly? Is there (or do I sense there will be) a high level of customer service? Are my visitors warmly greeted by staff when they arrive? Is the environment clean, orderly, and pleasant to be in?

Lobby Listing/Signage: Does the location have a lobby listing or directory of businesses? Can my business be included on this listing, so my visitors can receive extra assurance that this really is my business location? If I chose to use an office full time, will I be able to display corporate signage in and/or outside of the office?

No/Low Provider Branding: Does the provider display an overwhelming amount of branding in the space, which can confuse my guests, or is it kept to a minimum?

Administrative Support Services: If I need additional support, is there someone on staff to help me with presentations, documents, etc.? So that I never miss an important business call and to help with my corporate presence, is there the option of having a receptionist answer my calls and route them to me (or take a message) as needed?

Convenience Factors: I stressed earlier that this factor not only pertains to the convenience of the physical location for your prospects and clients, but also to the ease of your being able to access the services themselves. The extent that additional amenities improve the ease and enjoyment of use of the services (e.g., nearby dining, shopping, access to major roadways, etc.) should also be considered.

Location: Is the space in an area that is convenient to my clients, prospects, and me? Is it near major roadways, public transportation, or otherwise easy to travel to and from? Does the location have multiple locations that I can access, should my business needs take me to another area?

Parking: Is there parking available at the location for my visitors and me? What type of parking is available — surface, garage, or street? Is the parking ample or limited? Is it free or paid?

Accessibility: What are the provider's business hours? Am I able to access the services during the evenings or weekends or only during normal business hours? How easy and convenient is it for me to reserve a space? Will I be able to access all of the provider's spaces and services or are there limits to what I can use?

Available Amenities: What types of amenities are available at the location? Do I have the option of a furnished office or must I supply my own furniture? Are internet and telephone services available at an additional cost or are they included? Is there a copy/fax machine that I can access? Is there kitchen access with coffee, tea and/or other beverages and snacks?

Control Factors: This factor is all about your having control over how much or how little of an SOS service you use. Other ways to assess this include the scalability of the service — can you change or upgrade services as your business grows or fluctuates? Do you have to sign a long-term agreement or are short-term options available? How diverse are the service options that you have to choose from — many or limited?

> Diversity of Services: Does the location offer a variety of plans and services that I can choose from to fit my business needs?
>
> Flexible Agreement Terms: Are there flexible agreement terms that allow me to use space as I need it, or do I need to agree to a long-term commitment? What is the minimal usage requirement (e.g., an hour, a month)?
>
> Ease of Use: Can I easily change or upgrade services as my business grows or changes? Are there set-up fees or security deposits required to begin services? What is the cancellation policy?

TIME-SAVING TIP!
Print out *The 3 C's*™ evaluation grid at www.ldhoward.com.

***

These are the key factors that I have come across in my experience as a user of SOS and as a SOS provider, but if there are other criteria that are important to you, include them in the "Additional Notes" section on the evaluation grid and factor them in your final evaluation. For example, the types of other users at the location might be an important consideration for you — perhaps you don't want to be in a space where there are potential competitors, or maybe you'd prefer to work among others in the same industry.

You might have also noticed that pricing is not included as a factor in any of the categories. There are two primary reasons for this: 1) budgets are relative; and 2) I am an advocate of comparing on value and service, *not* price. Simply because a product or service is priced lower than a competitor's doesn't mean it provides a greater value. Conversely, just because a product or service is priced higher doesn't mean it's superior. That's why it's important to ask qualitative questions and evaluate your options along *The 3 C's*™ — you want the *best value* and *best service* that will fit your business needs.

Key Points:

1. *The 3 C's of Serviced Office Space*™ is a complete, unbiased guide for evaluating prospective SOS providers.

Action Exercises:

1. Print out *The 3 C's*™ evaluation grid by going to www.ldhoward.com.
2. Using the parameters discussed in this chapter, begin thinking about what you would want and/or need in a SOS provider for your business.

CHAPTER 7

FIVE SIMPLE STEPS

Now that you have a fuller appreciation of *The 3 C's*™ and how they can help you evaluate your SOS options, let's put this knowledge into action by discussing the five simple steps to help you cut costs, attract more clients, and improve your bottom line.

And just to add a tad more excitement, here's a fun mnemonic to help you easily remember these key steps: *B.R.I.S.K.*™

1. **B**rowse. Peruse the marketplace for SOS providers in the geographical area(s) of interest to you. The most efficient way to browse is by conducting an internet search, using relevant keywords such as "virtual office," "shared office," "office space," or "coworking."

2. **Research**. After identifying at least three locations in your desired area, perform a more in-depth review of each provider. To start, research each provider's *actual* street address to get more information about the location itself (e.g., demographics, accessibility, nearby amenities, etc.). Conduct additional research via the provider's website to see if there are photos of the facility, pricing details, and contact information to help you complete the next step.

3. **Interview**. Contact your top three provider prospects and let them know that you are interested in learning more about their services. The representative may invite you to tour the location; if so, take them up on the offer. If you are not invited to take a tour, ask to schedule one so that you can see the facility first hand, interview staff more thoroughly, and better determine if the prospective provider is a good fit for your needs. Remember to take *The 3 C's*™ evaluation grid with you and use it as a guide for asking questions and taking notes, being sure to fill in the SOS provider information at the top of the grid chart to help keep track.

 Don't be afraid to talk to the provider's clients while you are interviewing them. Yes, their clients may be working, but they may not mind being briefly interrupted to talk about how great the SOS provider is (or to tell you how much it sucks and to run as fast as you can)! If you're not able to speak with a client during the interview, ask the representative for client references.

At the close of your interview, ask for pricing information and the next steps to begin services if you decide to go with them. As I mentioned earlier, you may very well be able to get started on the same day if you want to.

4. **Select**. Once you've got all the information you need from the prospective location(s), evaluate your notes from *The 3 C's*™ evaluation grid and select the provider that is best for you. Be sure to read all of the provider's fine print before agreeing to anything and ask questions, if needed, so that you fully understand the terms of use.

5. **Kill The Rent.** Congratulations — you now have a Serviced Office Space to help grow your business! Start using your services right away so you can kill the rent and begin reaping the benefits of traditional commercial office space at a fraction of the cost. If you've selected to use an SOS provider as your company address, go ahead and update the address on your website, business cards, and other marketing

materials. If you've opted to have office or meeting room access, start scheduling client meetings in your new corporate office or conduct a training session in your new conference room. Your current and prospective clients will be impressed, and your bottom line will thank you!

Key Points:

- Remember to think B.R.I.S.K.™ when considering the five simple steps to cut costs, attract more clients, and improve your bottom line: browse, research, interview, select, and kill the rent.

Action Exercises:

1. Follow the five simple steps — B.R.I.S.K.™ — as discussed in this chapter for at least three SOS providers in your area.

2. If you haven't already done so, print out *The 3 C's*™ evaluation grid by going to www.ldhoward.com and use it as a guide when executing the five simple steps.

PART FOUR

HOW OTHERS HAVE KILLED THE RENT

*"Don't follow where the path may lead.
Go instead where there is no path
and leave a trail."
~Ralph Waldo Emerson*

HOW OTHERS HAVE KILLED THE RENT

We have definitely covered a lot in this book! More importantly, you now know a solution to help you operate your business with a professional image and the five simple steps to cut costs, attract more clients, and improve your bottom line.

In this part, I will provide some real-world case studies of how the SOS option can benefit small and large businesses. The case studies pull from businesses within different industries and with different needs — all to illustrate that regardless of where you may be in your business's life cycle, or whether you are faking it or not, SOS could be a viable option for you.[1]

---

[1] Please note that the solutions noted in the case studies reflect the nomenclature that I use for the packages I offer in my business. Though the services may be similar, the terminology used may vary from provider to provider.

THE CASE OF THE AUGMENTING AGENT

The Scenario
Steve has been an insurance agent for more than five years, and he's had a great deal of success. He has a list of happy clients, a pipeline full of prospects, and is one of the top performers each year. Because of the success he's had, he opened a small office a few years ago, enough for him to have his own private office, a ten-seat conference room to meet with clients and prospects, and a nice reception area for his secretary and guests. Steve likes his office, has a great relationship with the landlord, and can comfortably afford the rent.

The Challenge
To help grow his business, generate more income and serve more people, Steve wants to begin conducting workshops and group trainings. To start, he wants to have two-hour sessions two times per month with 50 people attending each session at a nominal admission fee of only $10 per person.

By doing this, Steve expects to educate and serve 100 more people per month and generate $1,000 in new revenue per month as follows:

Steve's Augmentation Strategy

50 Attendees per two-hour session
x 2 two-hour sessions per month
= 100 Attendees per month

x 10 Fee per attendee
= $1,000 Total new revenue generated

Though Steve's office is a great fit for his day-to-day administrative and other operational needs and the conference room is great for small sessions, he does not have enough space to accommodate attendees for the new sessions, so he's going to have to conduct the training sessions elsewhere.

Steve researches area hotels and finds that there are quite a few with rooms he can rent, but they require a minimum four-hour (half-day) block, and Steve only needs two hours max. Plus, the hotel won't allow him to bring snacks on the premises, and the hotel's caterer is expensive and doesn't offer the type of food and beverages he wants to provide. Steve also noticed that the hotel rates fluctuate quite significantly based on the day of the week, and the day he prefers to have the trainings is one of the higher rates. The lowest hotel rate he found was $500 for *one* training session, so he'd have to spend $1,000 for the two sessions he wants to hold each month — so every dollar he makes from the sessions will go directly to cover the hotel costs!

No Money for Steve

$500 Rate for a ½ day block at hotel
x 2 blocks needed per month
= $1,000 Cost for 2 sessions per month

$1,000 Revenue generated from sessions
($1,000) Less hotel costs
$0 No new revenue for Steve

The Solution
<u>A La Carte Training Room Use</u> — After reading *"Kill The Rent – Grow Your Biz"* and learning about SOS, Steve decided to follow the B.R.I.S.K.™ steps to see if it could work for him. Much to his surprise, he learned there was an SOS provider less than three miles from his office that has a training room he could rent for $75 per hour. Not only did the training room have enough space for his workshops, it included a projector that he could use for his presentation, the staff could arrange the room however he liked, and he was more than welcome to bring his own snacks. This was a far better solution for Steve to augment his business, as shown:

SOS Improves Steve's Bottom Line

$75 Hourly rate for training room
x 2 hours per session
= $150 Training room cost per session
= $300 Training room cost for 2 sessions

$1,000 Revenue generated from sessions
($300) Less training room costs
$700 Net monthly revenue gain for Steve

After all things considered, SOS was a far more convenient and flexible option for Steve. He was able to cut costs by more than 50%(versus using a hotel), attract more clients into his business, and improve his bottom line. Steve is now augmenting his business much more affordably than he imagined!

THE CASE OF THE TAXED ACCOUNTANT

The Scenario

After 15 years of working for a private accounting firm, April has decided to "go solo" and start her own accounting business. April has a small, but steady flow of clients whose taxes she does out of her home. She knows this is not the ideal solution, but she doesn't mind — her clients are family and friends that she's known for years and she's had them in her house many times before for social occasions.

The Challenge

One day, April decided to track how long it takes her to meet with each client. What she discovered is that it sometimes took her three hours to perform one client's work when she should have been able to do at least twice that many in the same amount of time. When looking closer, she realized that she and her clients were spending a great deal of time talking about non-work matters versus focusing on getting the task done. April was losing money because working out of her home was so comfortable — for her and her clients. Her friends and family were not taking her business seriously, and quite frankly, neither was she.

Ideal (Minimum)
Revenue Capacity of April's Tax Business

2 Clients seen per three-hour block
x 2 three-hour blocks per day (6-hour day)
= 4 Customers seen per day

x $50 Average fee per customer
= $200 Minimum revenue capacity per day
= $1,000 Minimum revenue capacity per week

Current Actual Revenue Activity
In April's Tax Business

1 Client seen per three-hour block
x 2 three-hour blocks per day (6-hour day)
= 2 customers seen per day

x $50 Average fee per customer
= $100 Actual revenue per day
= $500 Actual revenue per week

$1,000 Minimum revenue capacity per week
$500 Actual weekly revenue
($500) Missed weekly revenue opportunity

In addition to the mere fact that working out of her "free" home office was actually causing her to lose money, April wanted to broaden her clientele beyond those who she personally knew without breaking the bank. She knew that doing taxes or other accounting work at a coffee shop or other public venue was simply not an option because of the sensitivity of her work, so April contacted a commercial real estate agent to help her find a small office space. After weeks of searching, she wasn't able to find anything that would fit the budget she had set aside for office rent. April was at a loss and didn't know what to do.

The Solution

<u>Corporate Identity + 30-Hour Workspace Package</u>: A week later, April's agent suggested that she consider SOS, and suggested she read a book titled *"Kill The Rent – Grow Your Biz"* to see how the solution could work for her. April followed her agent's advice and the five steps in the book, and interviewed three SOS providers centrally located between where she lives and where the new clients she wants to attract live. She found a place that she really liked — the staff was professional and they had a variety of service plans that she could choose from, giving her control over her budget. April knew that when her clients began having their appointments here versus her home, they would know she was serious about her business and spend less time socializing. More importantly, April would take herself and her business more seriously, too.

April signed up for a plan that allowed her to use the SOS provider as her business address along with 30 hours of private office access, all for only $250 per month. She has since attracted more clients and grown her business because she is now meeting two to three clients in the same amount of time that it was taking her to meet just one in her home office.

The recaptured revenue more than covers the affordable fee she pays for SOS, which is far less than she would have paid by leasing a traditional commercial office space.

April Is No Longer Taxed

$500 Min. recaptured weekly revenue
$2,000 Min. recaptured monthly revenue
($250) Less monthly SOS cost
$1,750 Min. regained monthly revenue

What's even better, April didn't have to buy furniture, connect utilities, or be concerned about any of the other items she factored into her commercial office space budget — they were all included in with SOS! April was definitely able to cut costs, attract more clients, and improve her bottom line — and is no longer taxed for her accounting business!

THE CASE OF THE AGILE ATTORNEYS

The Scenario
Craig and Morgan have been partners in a successful law practice for more than 10 years. Having met in law school, they've always been the "yin" to the other's "yang," and this balance had worked well when meeting with potential new clients and persuading judges and juries in the courtroom. Their firm has earned a reputation for excellent results for their clients, has been featured on local news programs, and was named one of the top firms in their state.

The Challenge
Because of their successful track record and recent publicity, Craig and Morgan have been receiving an increasing number of prospective client requests from a neighboring state. In the past, requests from this state were relatively infrequent, so they didn't mind traveling intermittently to meet with a prospect at a colleague's office in that state or, when they weren't able to do that, to meet the client in the private dining room of a nice

restaurant. But now, with the increase in requests from this state, they have had to find a way to be more agile, open a new office, and manage growing their practice to meet this need without breaking the budget.

By Morgan's estimation, they would need a minimum of 1,000 square feet of space to open a new office, with three offices for two attorneys and a paralegal, a conference room, and reception area. She researched the average cost to lease a full-service[2] commercial space in the state and realized it would be extremely costly.

The Cost of Growth

$1,000 Minimum square footage needed
x 21 Average price per square foot
= $21,000 Annual rent in Year 1
= $1,750 Monthly rent in Year 1

Morgan also knew that in addition to the rent escalating by three percent each year and having to wait at least 60 days before the lease was finalized and they could actually open the new office, the firm would also need to spend at least another $5,000 up front to cover the security deposit, furnish the space, connect utilities and telephone lines, and purchase supplies and equipment. This was especially disconcerting especially given that she and Craig did not anticipate that the office would be utilized full time; essentially, they'd be paying a high

---

[2] With a full-service lease, utilities and janitorial services are typically included in the monthly rent.

price for space they did not need simply to have a presence in the state.

The Solution

Corporate Identity Package + A La Carte Private Office Use: After reading *"Kill The Rent – Grow Your Biz,"* Morgan suggested that she and Craig consider creating a satellite office in the other state via the SOS option. She explained that they can hold meetings in the state on an as-needed basis without the hassle of opening a physical office in the state. Instead, they can use the provider's address as their own for only $60 a month — this will give them a corporate presence in the state and any mail received can be forwarded to them in their home state.

When they need to use a private office or meeting room, they can reserve a room at the location for as little as $40 an hour — significantly less than the cost of a private dining room and without becoming a burden to the colleague who let them use their office in the past.

The Savings with Agility

$40 Hourly rate to reserve a private office
x 6 Hours per month, if needed
= $240 Monthly costs for private office usage
+ $60 Monthly amount for Corporate Identity
= $300 Maximum amount per month for SOS

$1,750 Monthly rent in traditional office space
$1,450 Monthly savings vs. traditional office space

Now, when the partners receive inquiries from the other state, they have a convenient location to meet with prospective and new clientele at a fraction of the cost of traditional commercial office space. Plus, as the firm's need for more hours grows, they can simply add more hours to their package or upgrade to a full-time office.

Indeed, SOS has given Craig and Morgan new found agility, and a better way to attract and serve more clients and improve their bottom line!

THE CASE OF THE CURTAILING COMPANY

The Scenario

A popular company has been in business for more than 40 years. Like any business that has been around this long, they have celebrated many successes and have survived and learned from many challenges along the way. The company has become a bit of a staple in the neighborhood and is considered to be a significant part of the childhood experience in their town. They do more than deliver an exceptional product for their customers; they create exceptional memories for them, too.

The Challenge

Although the company is very popular in the neighborhood, they've seen a steady decline in customers and revenues during the past couple of years for in-store transactions. The Chief Financial Officer (CFO) attributes this to the increase in online orders and a competitor who has moved into the area. The company is continuing to do well, but the rent is now becoming a larger percentage of their total expenses than they want it to be, so they have to figure out a way to curtail this cost while continuing to serve their loyal customers.

The Solution

<u>Full-Time Office Package</u> — The CFO recently saw an article about a book titled *"Kill The Rent – Grow Your Biz"* and how SOS can help the company to cut rent costs. After reading the book and taking its advice to heart, the CFO and Chief Executive Officer (CEO) developed a strategy that would enable them to reduce the company's rent costs and improve their bottom line.

Specifically, because the company's triple net[3] lease is up for renewal next year, the CFO negotiated new terms in which the company would only continue renting the space that's needed for their warehouse, reducing their square footage by more than half. The other half, about 1,800 square feet that is currently being used for administrative offices, can instead be housed at a SOS provider.

After following the B.R.I.S.K.™ steps discussed in the book, the company selected a SOS provider that had three adjacent offices they could use full time for their administrative offices. The company's full-time office package is inclusive of everything it needs to operate

---

[3] Unlike a full-service lease, in a triple net lease, the tenant is typically responsible for real estate taxes, building insurance, and maintenance (the three "nets") in addition to utilities and janitorial services.

efficiently: access to a conference room for presentations and meetings; access to a multi-function network printer; and the ability to transfer their current telephone system to the new administrative offices, enabling the change to remain completely seamless for their customers. The CFO also negotiated a monthly discount with the provider because they'd be using multiple offices, and the provider let them furnish the offices with their own furniture, saving the company additional money.

Further, because the provider offers administrative support services at a very competitive rate, the company's Administrative Assistant will now be able to focus on more strategic projects that will help to move the company forward, while the provider's administrative support services will be used for more routine tasks, such as making copies and basic document preparation.

All in all, the company was able to reduce their rent costs by more than 25% by simply relocating their administrative offices to a SOS provider:

Curtailed to Savings

1,800 Square feet currently used for admin offices
x $12 base rent per square foot
= $21,600 Annual base rent amount
= $1,800 Monthly base rent amount
+ $300 Monthly amount for utilities & janitorial
= $2,100 Total current monthly amount

$1,500 3 SOS admin offices @ $500 each
$600 Monthly savings by using SOS
$7,200 Annual savings by using SOS

By following the advice in *"Kill The Rent – Grow Your Biz"*, the company was able to cut costs, continue serving new and current customers and reinvest the savings — $7,200 a year — into their business!

NOW GO... KILL THE RENT & GROW YOUR BIZ!

"When the record book on you is finished, let it show your wins and your losses. But don't let it show that you didn't try."
~Jim Rohn

NOW GO ... KILL THE RENT & GROW YOUR BIZ!

I want to applaud you for reading this book as a step toward moving your business forward, and I truly hope that you have enjoyed the journey we've taken together.

I hope that this book has encouraged you. I hope that this book has motivated you. I hope that this book has inspired you. But most importantly, I hope that this book has reminded you of how fortunate you are to be a small-business owner, and in a position to chart the course of your future.

But the question that remains now is — *"So what?"*

Even though you now know how and why you have been faking it, the risks of doing so, and a viable solution that could potentially change the trajectory of your small business for the better — none of it matters if you don't take *action*.

I know it may seem scary, not because it's difficult — but because it's new and unfamiliar. But I can assure you that once you transition from working out of your home or a public venue to a more professional environment, you will wonder what took you so long.

By reading this book, you now have a new awareness of how to start killing the rent and growing your business. You have been armed with information and equipped with tools to help you start attracting more clients and improving your bottom line.

You've learned what Serviced Office Space is, its benefits and challenges, a way to evaluate different provider options in the marketplace, and five simple steps to get started.

But it is all for naught if you don't make a decision and take action today. In the words of Amelia Earhart, "The most difficult thing is the decision to act, the rest is mere tenacity."

Now is the time for you to put the information and solutions discussed in this book into action. If you have been faking it, want a more professional way to conduct business, want to attract more clients, or want to improve your bottom line, the answer is literally in front you.

The next step is up to you.

THANK YOU FOR READING THIS BOOK!

I would love to hear what you have to say
and would appreciate your feedback.

Your input could help to make the next version
of this book even better.

**Please leave a helpful review on Amazon and share
this book with anyone else who could use it.**

Thank you so much!
L.D. Howard

HOW CAN I HELP YOU?

I'd love to learn more about your business
goals and help you succeed!

Please visit www.ldhoward.com
to continue the discussion.

ABOUT THE AUTHOR

LaTaunya "L.D." Howard was born on the 4th of July in Washington, DC. She grew up in the DC suburbs along with her father, mother, older brother, and the family's pet Pekingese, "Ziggy."

At an early age, LaTaunya's parents encouraged her to pursue her artistic interests — including ballet, tap, jazz dancing, and toe dancing. LaTaunya won many awards for her dancing, and later expanded her artistic interests to musical instruments, including the clarinet and oboe. As a teenager, LaTaunya began taking piano lessons, and briefly attended the Duke Ellington School of the Performing Arts. After transferring to a different high school, LaTaunya played piano accompaniment for the school's gospel choir and later enrolled in college majoring in Arts Management.

During her sophomore year of college, LaTaunya changed her focus, eventually earning a Bachelor's in Political Science and a Master's in Public Administration. LaTaunya, always having an analytical mind, used her education to build a 15+ year career in financial management with the state, local and federal government. It was through one of these opportunities that LaTaunya was first exposed to entrepreneurship as a financial consultant for a quasi-governmental agency.

LaTaunya enjoyed working as a self-employed financial consultant, but due to the events of September 11, 2001, and the financial uncertainties that followed, LaTaunya returned to working with the government later that year. Around the same time, LaTaunya was also pursuing a private pilot's license (and had already completed ground school) but put this goal on hold after the airport where she was training was temporarily shut down after the events of September 11.

Despite returning to the workforce as an employee in late 2001, LaTaunya never lost that entrepreneurial "itch." Entrepreneurship helped LaTaunya realize that she enjoys educating and working with business owners. So, in 2012, she began using her talents and experience to teach at the college level (one of her "bucket list" items) and to open Howard Corporate Centre, LLC, a Serviced Office Space supporting small businesses. After expanding her business in 2015, LaTaunya later added commercial real estate to her service portfolio as another way to add value to business owners. Then, as a way to close the knowledge gap about Serviced Office Space that she observed exists among many business owners, LaTaunya decided to write *Kill The Rent – Grow Your Biz* to educate them about how it can help them achieve their business goals.

LaTaunya lives in Maryland, and has never forgotten her artistic roots. She patrons the John F. Kennedy Center for the Performing Arts, where she once served on the Circles Board, and enjoys playing her baby grand piano, which she affectionately calls "Mimi." And every time LaTaunya is at an airport or sees a plane soaring through the air, she's reminded that becoming a private pilot must soon be checked off of her "bucket list" too.

REFERENCES

---

[i] U.S. Small Business Administration, Office of Advocacy (2017). *Interest Rates and Non-Bank Lending to Small Businesses [PDF]*.

[ii] U.S. Small Business Administration, Office of Advocacy (2016). *Small Business Finance Frequently Asked Questions [PDF]*.

[iii] U.S. Small Business Administration, Office of Advocacy (n.d.). *Survival Rates and Firm Age [PDF]*.

[iv] Lavoie, L. (2014, April 24). Entrepreneur helps clients with work space. *The Laurel Leader*, p. 12.

[v] Brown, J. (n.d.). *How Important Are Small Businesses to Local Economies?* Retrieved from http://smallbusiness.chron.com/important-small-businesses-local-economies-5251.html.

[vi] Headd, B. (n.d.). *The Role of Microbusinesses in the Economy [PDF]*. U.S. Small Business Administration, Office of Advocacy.

[vii] Altgerowitz, R., & Zonderman, J. (2007). *Financing Your Business Made Easy*. Madison, WI: Entrepreneur Media Inc.

[viii] Ibid.

[ix] Mansfield, M. (2016, November 01). *Startup Statistics – The Numbers You Need to Know*. Retrieved from https://smallbiztrends.com/2016/11/startup-statistics-small-business.html

[x] Wood, M. (2014, July 14). *The Truth About SBA Loans*. Retrieved from http://www.foxbusiness.com/features/2014/07/14/truth-about-sba-loans.html.

[xi] Osnabrugge, M. V., & Robinson, R. J. (2000). *Angel investing: matching startup funds with startup companies: the guide for entrepreneurs, individual investors, and venture capitalists*. San Francisco: Jossey-Bass.

[xii] Kohler, M. J. (2015, June 04). 3 Ways to Bring On a Silent Partner. Retrieved from https://www.entrepreneur.com/article/244633#

[xiii] What SBA Doesn't Offer | The U.S. Small Business Administration. (n.d.). Retrieved from https://www.sba.gov/loans-grants/see-what-sba-offers/what-sba-doesnt-offer

[xiv] U.S. Small Business Administration, Office of Advocacy (2016). *Small Business Finance Frequently Asked Questions [PDF]*.

[xv] What are the pros and cons of crowdfunding? (2014, November 12). Retrieved from https://www.crowdcrux.com/pros-and-cons-of-crowdfunding

[xvi] Altgerowitz, R., & Zonderman, J. (2007). *Financing Your Business Made Easy*. Madison, WI: Entrepreneur Media Inc.

[xvii] Ibid.

[xviii] Osnabrugge, M. V., & Robinson, R. J. (2000). *Angel investing: matching startup funds with startup companies: the guide for entrepreneurs, individual investors, and venture capitalists*. San Francisco: Jossey-Bass.

[xix] U.S. Small Business Administration, Office of Advocacy (2016). *Small Business Finance Frequently Asked Questions [PDF]*.

[xx] Ibid.

[xxi] Ibid.

[xxii] Ibid.

[xxiii] Ibid.

[xxiv] Mansfield, M. (2016, November 01). *Startup Statistics – The Numbers You Need to Know*. Retrieved from https://smallbiztrends.com/2016/11/startup-statistics-small-business.html

[xxv] Should You Use Your Home Address for Business? | QuickBooks | Should You Use Your Home Address for Business? (2017, May 19). Retrieved from https://quickbooks.intuit.com/r/compliance-licensing/should-you-use-your-home-address-for-your-business/

[xxvi] Rise Of The Shared Workplace In The Sharing Economy. (n.d.). Retrieved from http://www.reuters.com/brandfeatures/cbre/workplace

[xxvii] White, D. A. (2017, June 08). 4 Ways Coworking Spaces Inspire Innovation and Collaboration. Retrieved from https://www.entrepreneur.com/article/295289

[xxviii] Mathur, N. (2017, August 23). Did Starbucks miss the co-working boat? Retrieved from https://e27.co/starbucks-miss-co-working-boat-20170823/

[xxix] J. (2013, June 14). Virtual Offices Can Make Your Business Greener. Retrieved from https://eco-officegals.com/virtual-offices-can-make-your-business-greener/

[xxx] Do You Need a Physical Address For Your Business? (2016, October 28). Retrieved from https://www.legalzoom.com/articles/do-you-need-a-physical-address-for-your-business

www.ingramcontent.com/pod-product-compliance
Lightning Source LLC
Chambersburg PA
CBHW071044240526
45471CB00014B/565